SORRY
I BARFED ON YOUR BED

SORRY
I BARFED ON YOUR BED

(and Other Heartwarming Letters from Kitty and Doggie)

JEREMY GREENBERG

Andrews McMeel
Publishing®

Kansas City • Sydney • London

For my wonderful mother-in-law, Arlene

From: Sukie
Age: 5 Years
Re: I heard there was a reward for a lost shoe

Dear Pack Leader,

I couldn't help but notice you running around the house frantically looking for one of your $200 running shoes. Perhaps I can be of assistance. I smelled, er, uh, saw the shoe buried under my dog toys. In situations like these, it's best not to ask questions and just be thankful to have the shoe back. Unfortunately, I can't guarantee its condition. When shoes that smell so scrumptiously like Pack Leader's feet are abducted, they often have some bite or chew marks. If you find that the shoe is damaged beyond use, I will graciously accept it as my reward for returning it to you.

Love,
Sukie

Dear Pack Leader,

Thank you for throwing this ball into the lake! I love retrieving it almost as much as I love shaking frigid lake water all over you afterward. And even though it's not a duck, I will still enjoy sneaking it into the house later to rip off its fuzz.

    Some doggies have to learn to swim, but I was bred to retrieve. So if you ever get bored, just know that in addition to fetching a tennis ball from a lake, I will gladly dive for rubber rings in a swimming pool, fetch stones out of the ocean, snatch the baby's bath toys from the tub, and even remove those big, funny goldfish from the neighbor's little pond.

Love,
Samson

From: Samson
Age: 4 Years
Re: Honestly, I was gonna jump in whether you threw the ball or not

From: Gandalf
Age: 2 Years
Re: Maybe I have one in my purse

Dear Pack Leader,

What is that thing with four legs that just walked by us on the ground? It smelled like another doggie, but that can't be—it wasn't being carried around in a leather purse. Is it true that some doggies aren't allowed to go on airplanes? What about the rumor that not all doggies eat standing on a dining room table? That sounds too impossible to be true. And please tell me those stories about doggies who pull people through the snow are just tales told to puppies at night before they go to sleep on their pillow-top mattress doggie beds. I mean, humans pulling doggies makes sense. You carry me everywhere. But a doggie hauling around humans? Do you know how big of a purse you'd need?

Love,
Gandalf

Dear Sprinkler Head,

First of all, I respect you as I respect all great adversaries. Sprinkler Head is second only to Vacuum Cleaner in terms of ferocity. No matter how hard Jewel bites Sprinkler Head's stream of water, Sprinkler Head keeps turning and sprinkling. My pack leader says I'm a dumb doggie, that Jewel can never figure out Sprinkler Head's tactics. But she underestimates Sprinkler Head. I'm always surprised when Sprinkler Head pops out of the ground. Sprinkler Head waits till I'm stuck in crouching potty position, knows I'm vulnerable for attack, then pops out of the ground and Sprinkler Head does business on Jewel while Jewel does business on lawn.

But we're not finished, Sprinkler Head. One day I will bite your stream of water just right and you will shut off and retreat, knowing that Jewel has victoriously defended herself against an irrigation system.

Your worthy opponent,
Jewel

From: Jewel

Age: 12 Years

Re: I see we meet again, Sprinkler Head

From: Mr. P Nut
Age: 12 Years
Re: That's Mr. P Nut to you

Dear Beloved Pack Leader,

Why am I so grumpy? Because despite my name clearly being Mr. P Nut, just as it says on my tag, you and the rest of the pack repeatedly laugh as you call me Mr. P-Diddy Dingleberry, Nutsy-P Nutter, Mr. Pee-pee Nut, The Vet Cut Off His P Nuts, Mr. P Nuts and Popcorn, Mr. P Has Gone Nuts, and perhaps the worst of all, Mr. Allergic to P Nuts. You know I love you, Pack Leader, but think about how you'd feel if instead of calling you Marsha I called you Swamp Marsha, Drain the Marsha, or Damp Marsha? You'd be sitting on the grass making an adorably grumpy face as well.

My great granpaw, the original Mr. P Nut (who spelled it Peaznutten until he went through Ellis Island) came to this country in search of a better dog park. And I am proud to have the Mr. P Nut name.

I understand you can't undo years of calling me names like Mr. P Nutty Nutcracker overnight. But if you ask me if I want a cookie, I think that we can start the healing process.

Love,
Mr. P Nut the Third, Esq.

Dear Pack Leader,

Even though I'm a little puppy, I know my manners. If someone's kind enough to pour you a glass of red stuff, you should drink it. Normally German shepherds aren't into red drink, but I know humans have it all the time, so it would be rude of me not to at least taste it. So far I've tasted down to the length of my tongue. I left the rest for you, because I know it's nice to share.

If you want to go back in the kitchen and get me a, how do you say, *sandwich*, I will politely sample that as well.

Love,

Kellan

From: Kellan
Age: 3 Months
Re: Well, if you insist

From: Marley
Age: 2 Years
Re: Piggy told me what you said about me

Dear Pack Leader,

Just because I'm happy-go-lucky by nature doesn't mean I don't have feelings. Piggy told me that you said you thought I was cuter as a puppy. Well, I'm sure there are people who thought you were cuter when you were younger. But if I was your puppy back then, I wouldn't say mean things about you if you suddenly grew a fatty tumor on your hind leg, or only had eyebrows over one eyeball. I could look past your mangy appearance and see your inner beauty.

This has made me so sad that Piggy and I are refusing to get out of bed this morning. I know you have to go to work, but you really hurt my feelings. It's not like you're a spring chicken (or I'd eat you—spring chicken is Marley's favorite flavor of dog food).

Piggy says you owe me an apology. And please apologize soon. I really have to pee.

Love,
Marley

Dear Beloved Beta,

Okay, I'll go over the rules one more time: First I bring you the ball, then you say, "Out!" which I think means "tug." You try to remove the ball from my mouth while I clench down. Then you repeat, "Out, Lua" while I completely fail to understand you, and maybe also let out a few playful growls. Then you say, "Lua, let go" while I wag my tail because I heard my name. Finally, after you give up and let go, I make sure the ball is drenched in slobber and then drop it in your lap, just to grab it away again when you reach for it.

    Please try to keep up! This is an important game that helps us establish pack order, and I can't continue to outrank you if you won't play.

Love,
Lua

From: Lua
Age: 4 Years
Re: You can take the ball, but I want you to earn it

From: Mel
Age: 6 Years
Re: Don't clean the house—I just stank it up!

Dear Pack Leader,

I don't spend all day putting my adorable Mel stink all over the carpet so you can run in here with your loud windbag friend and remove it. Don't you want people to know that you have a dog the moment they walk in the door? I work very hard to make sure that everything you own smells like Mel. As your doggie, it's my job to provide an environment that profoundly stinks like an old mutt who hasn't had a bath in six months. I would appreciate a bit of consideration for the work I do.

Oh, and make sure you leave your shoes on when you come in this house, so I know where you've been!

Love,
Smelly Mel

Dear Pack Leader,

Look, we all have days when things don't go smoothly. I know that you're embarrassed. I can see you turning away and trying to pretend I'm someone else's doggie. But this is no different than when you're in the bathroom and have to yell out for someone to bring you more toilet paper. I don't pretend to not know you when that happens. In fact, I try to get into the bathroom when the door opens just to hang out with you in your time of need.

And this doesn't mean we have to go to the vet. I don't have impacted anal glands, and I don't have worms. I don't have an allergy, and I don't have a tick.

I just have poor timing.

Why don't you stop hiding your face, grab some leaves, and give me a hand.

Love,
Your Frogdog

From: Frogdog
Age: 6 Years
Re: A clean break with the past

From: Macy
Age: 7 Months
Re: We never go out anymore (and I'm sorry I pooped in your shoe)

Dear Pack Leader,

I'll never forget the day you adopted me. You looked at me and said, "Yes. This one will work." And it was wonderful. We used to go out all the time. You'd come home from work and look me in the eyes and say, "Okay, Macy. Do your magic." And we'd walk by all the cute girls at the coffee shops and the yogurt shops. And then one day a woman bent down to scratch my cute head and said, "Hi. I'm Penny." Ever since, you and Penny have been like kibbles and bits. But I barely get a ball thrown at me and am no longer allowed on your bed. I am beginning to feel like you used me just to get a girlfriend! You probably even named me Macy just because women like that department store.

I'm not asking you to leave Penny in the car on a hot day. But since we never go out anymore, I didn't think you'd mind if I pooped in your shoe.

Love,
Macy

Dear Pack Leader,

Did you hear that? There's a ghost in the closet! I know you said, "Jasper, relax. It's just something that fell." But why would something just fall? After I'm done being surprised, I will bark and growl at it again. I know you said, "Jasper, it's just a jacket sliding off the hanger. Stop barking and chew on your bone." But who can chew at a time like this? I wonder if it's the same ghost who you're convinced is just the ice maker. It would make sense—it's got to get cold making all that ice, so the ghost probably needs a jacket.

Love,
Jasper

From: Jasper
Age: 6 Months
Re: This house is haunted!

From: Jane
Age: 11 Years
Re: I love the smell of summer and a decomposing squirrel

Dear Pack Leader,

Here's a bit of advice: If you want people to like you, then you have to routinely rub your body on decaying animals. For example, if you have a hot date, nothing beats a good roll in the festering remains of a squirrel. It's an immediate attention getter! For family functions, I recommend mashing your fur into the putrid carcass of a dead bird. Its delicate aroma will not be immediately noticeable when you trot into the room, but you'll soon leave everyone breathless! A good workplace stench shouldn't be too strong, so go with a bit of dead mouse. It will provide just a hint of gag-inducing funk, yet still leave everyone asking, "What did you roll in?"

And please don't feel self-conscious if you don't stink like a festering rodent. I still love you.

Love,
Jane

Dear Pack Leader,

Why do I look so adorably sad? Because I clearly heard you tell one of the younger pack members to *park* it! Then you told an older pack member that you were going to teach him how to parallel *park*, after you finished watching your favorite movie, *Gosford Park*. Every doggie knows what the word *park* means. Yet, you don't seem to be putting your shoes on. I even did my flailing French bulldog sprint to the door, complete with a near hyperventilating pant. But you just looked at me and asked, "What is it, Ozzy? Chill out."

Sure, Ozzy will chill. It's okay. And the next time you say, "Ozzy, come," I'll ignore you because I'm sure you just meant "I'd like some gum."

Love,
Ozzy

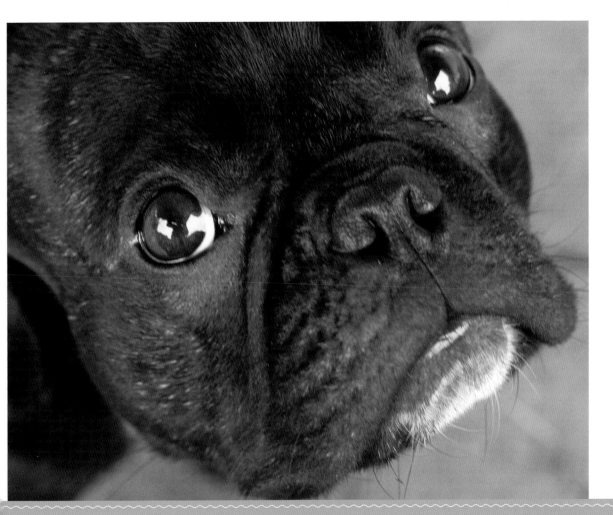

From: Ozzy
Age: 1 Year
Re: Yes, I would love to go to the *parallel park*!

From: Mario
Age: 4 Years
Re: My pack leader kindly requests that you get off her ass

Dear Other Pack Leader,

I'm introducing myself because, according to my pack leader, you are riding our asses so closely that you must want to get to know us. Well, I want to get to know you, too! My pack leader also says we're surrounded by idiots. Nice to meet you, idiot! My name's Mario.

I love learning about other people. You must be very educated, because all of my pack keeps asking who in the hell taught you how to drive. I wish I could drive, but I'm a doggie.

This traffic jam is a lot of fun. It's like a dog park for cars. It's neat to see so many people who, according to my pack leader, drive with their heads up their asses. What a great way to get to know yourself!

Love,
Mario

Howdy, Beta Buddy,

Whatcha doin'? Me, I'm in the backyard. Alpha sent me out here because she said she was trying to clean. So, then I stuck my nose through the knot in the piece of fence and chatted with the neighbor's dog for a while. But then someone yelled, "Shut up, Bernie!" and the other dog went inside its house. Then I climbed onto the sun chair and napped for a bit, until I heard the door open, and I figured Alpha must've thrown you out, too. So I was thinking that we should totally hang. If you're going to wash your car, I am more than happy to attack the hose. If you want to cut the grass, I can walk behind you and bark at the mower. Are you going to put up Christmas lights? I can make you nervous by running back and forth under the ladder. Come on, Beta. I wanna do something! I'm bored, man! I even offered Alpha to help clean the house, but apparently licking the metal banister had already been done.

Love,
Bernie

From: Bernie
Age: 8 Years
Re: Howdy, Beta Buddy

From: Sammy
Age: 2 Years
Re: Always leave 'em smiling

Dear Pack Leader,

I just want to take a moment and let you know how lucky I am to have such a thoughtful companion. Most doggies have to hunt leaves one by one. But you conveniently rake them into little hills all around the yard. You even yell, "Sammy, I just raked those!" to let me know that they're ready for me to jump into and rescatter all over the yard. And you further cheer me on by yelling, "Sammy, come on!"

You know, I used to get a bit jealous when you'd set out warm, clean clothes fresh from the dryer for the cat to sit on. But that's just one pile of clothes. You must've made like four or five piles of leaves for me! I will show my gratitude later by barking at the doorbell while the kids are napping. In the meantime, I'll go in the house while you re-rake the leaves.

Love,
Sammy

Dear Pack Leader Dearest,

I'm sorry I didn't make Prima Doggie Ballerina, Mama. I'll try harder, I promise. I know that you had a bright future as a dancer until you decided to settle down and adopt puppies. You gave it all up for me, and one day I'll get that lead in the *Pupcracker* and make you so proud. I don't wanna go to the park like the other puppies my age. I have an opportunity to be something, just like you used to. I'll work extra hard to balance on my hind legs when you hold a piece of hot dog above my nose. It's the least I can do for your getting me this beautiful tutu.

Love,
Camilla

From: Camilla
Age: 8 Months
Re: Purina Ballerina

From: T-Bone
Age: 15 Months
Re: Studies show that families who eat together are happier

Dear Pack Leader,

Quick question: When you were growing up did your mommy make you eat on a welcome mat by yourself in a corner of the house? Bet not. She probably set your bowl on the table next to the other pack members. So why do you make me eat alone on the floor like I'm some kind of dog?

I love you, and I'm a pack animal. I'm not some antisocial cat or serial killer. I would very much appreciate it if you placed my bowl next to yours. It's important to my self-esteem. Plus, doggies who don't get to eat with humans are at greater risk of becoming Alpoholics. So please let me sit with you during dinner, or I'll spend the rest of my life thinking that I'm just some pet.

Love,

T-Bone

Dear Pack Leader,

For a limited time only, I will be giving out free dog kisses. This is a special promotion, so don't wait. The details are as follows: Anyone who is part of my pack who happens to walk too closely to me will be given one free, remarkably sloppy dog kiss on her leg. Any baby crawling by me on the ground will be given a slobbery kiss across his face, as well as near the mouth—just in case there are any spare food crumbs. Pack members who fall asleep with their feet sticking out of a blanket will receive free, ticklishly-yucky toe kisses. And anyone who lets me sit on her lap will be given a big, wet, spittle-filled smooch.

Remember to act now! This special only lasts until you say, "Samuel, that is sooooo disgusting. Knock it off!"

Love,
Samuel

From: Samuel
Age: 7 Years
Re: Free dog kisses for a limited time only

From: Spike
Age: 6 Years
Re: Help me help you

Dear Pack Leader,

You look tired! You know what helps my tail wag after a long day of not being near you? Repeatedly dropping Squeak Doggie-Dog in your lap until you look at me and yell, "How many times do I have to throw this nasty thing?!" Every day you leave for what in dog years feels like a week. I get to stay home and gnaw on Squeakeezy. But you have to be away at someplace that makes your shoes smell like cheap carpet. I bet you dream about throwing this toy for me all day long. Well, I am not the kind of doggie who will just walk away after having my Squeak Doggie-Dog thrown once! I love you! And I won't stop bringing you the Squeak-O Double D until you scream, "Enough, Spike!" and throw it in a drawer.

Then I'll just stare at you.

Love,
Spike

Dear Pack Leader,

Since I'm your "Am I ready to have a baby?" tester puppy, I thought you'd appreciate a brief progress report:

You call me "Dodger Wodger" about 7.5 times per day—an excellent level of cutesy baby talk! I can really see you doing that to a human baby and it actually caring, even if you didn't have a cookie in your hand. And you've already set up playdates with the next-door neighbor's puppy. That is thoughtful but not necessary. Since that doggie and I are neighbors, I can assure you that unless you reinforce every piece of the shared fence, that puppy and I will have many playdates without your having to arrange them.

Obviously you're doing an amazing job with toys and blankets. This fuzzy banana thing is at exactly my sleep number. And while this stuffed-crab toy's a bit weird, I'm guessing it was a gift from a well-meaning uncle who works at the seafood counter of a grocery store, so I'm willing to let it go.

So keep up the great work! I'd say right now the only difference between me and a human baby is my ability to tap a paw on the back door when I need to go potty.

Love,
Baby Dodger

From: Dodger

Age: 12 Weeks

Re: Human baby simulation almost complete

From: Mousse

Age: 3 Years

Re: It doesn't have to be like this; you're making a mistake

Dear Wannabe Groomer Pack Leader,

Can we talk about this? I'm not that dirty, I promise! I know some doggies love baths. But some doggies also eat their own poop. If I'd known this was why you called me, I would've gone limp and forced you to drag me into the tub. I can't believe I didn't see this coming. I guess your starting to brush me should've been my first clue. When I saw the towels, I thought that maybe you were taking a bath. That's fine. I'll wait outside the tub and lick the water off of your legs when you get out. But then you pulled out the giant orange bottle of doggie soap, with that dumb smiling bulldog.

    That bulldog on the cover of the shampoo bottle seems happy to be bathed because she doesn't have a naturally shiny, beautiful coat. Most bulldogs aren't into appearance. But Mousse is a pretty doggie! Please don't give me a bath. My fur will get so dry and frizzy that you'll think I'm a Lakeland terrier.

Love,
Mousse

Dear Pack Leader,

Why are you constantly yelling, "Stella! Stella! Stop barking!"? I bark way less than the rest of the pack. Other pack members are always barking about how their day in school was, or for me to stop drinking from the toilet. But I bark only when I absolutely have to: like when I have to use the potty, when I want my breakfast, or when the doorbell rings, or another dog walks by the house, or the cat gives me a dirty look from atop the staircase, or I see my reflection in a mirror, or Timmy falls down a well, or if I need to practice my singing for the next full moon.

I'm practically giving you the silent treatment.

Love,
Stella

From: Stella
Age: 6 Years
Re: I think the mail's here!

From: Max
Age: 18 Months
Re: You said, "Not on the couch." This *isn't* the couch.

Dear Pack Leader,

I don't know why you're looking at me like that. I clearly recall you saying, "Max, get off the couch!" And that's why I'm on the recliner. I know you didn't expect me to curl up on the floor. It's covered in dog hair. Yuck! But this recliner has no hair on it, and it smells like you—my favorite smell in the whole world.

Please don't make me get down. Do you know how much work it was to get up here? I forgot this is a rocking chair, and when I jumped up the first time, it flew backward and scared the crap out of me. I had to growl at the chair for an hour before trying again. And now that I've finally settled in, I really do not want to get down—unless I can have a spot on the couch.

Love,

Max

Dear Pack Leader,

Seriously, I totally thought this was one of my Beggin' Strips. Whoops! Honest mistake. I know that I am only allowed to eat from your plate when you're in the other room. But here you are, right in front of me, and boy do I almost have egg on my face.

This is really just a big misunderstanding. I would never take something that I thought was yours if I thought you'd catch me. In the future, I will try to do a better job listening for the difference between the sound your shoes make on the kitchen linoleum and on the family room's hardwood. I apologize for being caught stealing your bacon, and I promise not to get caught in the future.

Love,

Babe

From: Babe
Age: 2 Years
Re: Let's play "Steal the Bacon"

From: Doll
Age: 14 Years
Re: The scent of a woman

Dear Beloved Pack Leader,

I know I shouldn't be on the bed, but I just want to sleep in your wonderful scent. Not every doggie has a leader who smells of Paris Hilton brand perfume and Lady Speed Stick, and I want to enjoy it! You always make me sleep on the little bed on the floor, and I like that bed—don't get me wrong. It even has my name embroidered on it. But it smells like cedar chips. My pack leader is not a tree!

   You clearly aren't aware of how delightful it is to sleep in another doggie's funk, or you'd let me on the bed with you every night. That's why I'm rubbing myself on your sheets. Now, when you go to bed tonight, all you'll be able to think about is me.

Love,

Doll

Dear Pack Leader,

I know what you're thinking, but this isn't just another one of my yearly attempts to enjoy the cheesy popcorn that Uncle Karl sends at Christmas. I actually have a surprise for you! I'm training to be a Seeing Eye dog. I know there are schools for that. But first, I thought putting this tin on my head would help me understand what it's like not to see. The fact that there were cheesy popcorns at the bottom, which I did eat, was purely a coincidence.

Now if you'd be so kind, please help me get this thing off my head, or I'll need my own guide dog to keep from banging into the couch.

Love,
Dante

From: Dante
Age: 15 Years
Re: It's not what it looks like

From: Raisin

Age: 18 Months

Re: That bag of feathers was, like, impossible to open

Dear Pack Leader,

You know, as pack leaders go, you don't get enough credit for the small things you do to make me happy. Even when you don't say, "You wanna go, Raisin?" and take me with you, you know that I'll get bored alone, so you graciously leave a homemade bag of feathers for me to play with. Thank you!

But if you don't mind a bit of constructive criticism, you really should've left one side of the bag open. I had to tear at it for like an hour to get to the feathers. Only after digging my rear claws into the couch as an anchor was I finally able sever the bag that I've watched you work on ever since Raisin was a little puppy Raisinette.

Also, for the next feather bag you make me, can you leave the feathers on the bird?

Love,
Raisin

My Lady,

Since domestic kitties shredded their first rolls of ancient Egyptian toilet papyrus, we have earned our keep by ridding homes of pests. We have banished mice from barns and feather dusters from tables. We have scoured windowsills for half-dead flies, terrorized untied shoelaces, and even made our force known to the tails of sleeping puppy dogs. And now, my human, allow me to protect you from the latest scourge: red laser dots.

We do not know where these red dots come from. Some suspect they live in a penlike object. That's why kitties knock all pens off countertops—to stop the red dot menace before it starts. And we know they make you nervous, because every time they appear and we swat them, you laugh.

But never fear; I will fight the red dot whenever it appears, even if it leads me right into a wall and I bump my head.

Love,
Hendrix

Name: Hendrix
Age: 3½ Years
Re: Stand back, my liege, the red dot attacks

Name: Tippy
Age: 5 Months
Re: Tippy has two mommies

Dear Two-legged Mommy with No Tail,

I know that it's wrong to purr for one parent more than another, but you could learn a few things from Furry Mommy. First of all, Furry Mommy never shoos me off her bed. But you hog your big bed all to yourself—and you don't even have your name embroidered on it. And when I do try to climb back onto your bed, rather than throw me off like you do, Furry Mommy climbs up with me if you're not looking. Furry Mommy also understands the importance of having dinner together as a family. Any time you refill my bowl, Furry Mommy runs right up and eats my cat food with me. But you eat alone at the kitchen table. When I try to jump up to join you, you say, "Get down, Tippy!" Furry Mommy lets me bite her ears, and she likes to play chase. All you like to do is take pictures of me wearing baby bonnets.

But you do make the food appear, and even as a kitty I understand that someone has to wear the pants in this family. The last time you tried to put pants on Furry Mommy, she whined and shook her legs 'til the pants fell off.

Love,
Tippy

Dear Insomniac,

I totally know what you mean when you say it's hard to get a good night's sleep (especially with me purring in your ear). I mean, the only places I can really get any rest are the wheel wells of cars, flowerpots, the neighbor's doghouse, the toaster oven if left open, most backpacks, underneath a lawn mower, a dry sink, a warm backyard fence, sock drawers, that bag you keep your wedding dress in, an evacuated underground bee's nest, an old suitcase, the branches of a Christmas tree, this banister, or any flat surface. It's torture.

Love,
Dakota

Name: Dakota
Age: 8 Years
Re: Don't wake me! I'm dreaming of new places to sleep

Name: Ili
Age: 3½ Years
Re: I hope there's no MSG—it makes my tongue feel sandpapery

Dear Kitty Restaurant Owner,

Let me begin my review of your establishment by complimenting you on the cat-friendly atmosphere. Most restaurants pretentiously serve food on a table, and you can only get a taste when the human becomes distracted or gets up to use the potty. I've even been thrown off a table for checking the temperature of a dish with my tail! It's enough to make you feel like you weren't allowed to eat from the same plate. But the way you dumped the food right on the floor made me feel like I was the only one who would be eating it.

The service was also very nice. Normally, when food is served, they say, "Bon appétit." But when this food was dropped, you said, "Son of a bitch!"—even though I saw no puppies.

As for the cat food itself, while I did like the pile of worms, I couldn't tell if they were savory chicken, beef, liver, or seafood flavor. And I was disappointed that the green things were not lizards. But they were covered in a yummy sauce, so I was able to lick them at least.

All in all, I thought it was a nice dining experience. The only major recommendation is that the server should've also dropped a fortune cookie at the end of the meal, so that I'd have something to bat around.

Love,
Ili

Dear Adoption Lawyer,

Theodora and I have been together for as far back as I can remember, which, if cat memory serves me correctly, is about sixteen hours. Where did we meet? I know it's going to sound cliché, but we met online—by which I mean we were *lying on* the bed. When our eyes met, we just stared at each other—she was so taken by me that she never even blinked. Junior was also there, but he'd fallen over. I strolled up, sniffed her, and groomed her ear. She was speechless. Luckily, I happen to be into the soft, silent type.

Theodora's not that affectionate, but I know she loves me. And she is not possessive at all. She never asks me where I've been, or why I smell like goldfish. And Junior? I've never met a better-behaved kitten in all my life. That's why I'd like to adopt him. I know his mother wants him to have a stable male influence— and you can't get more stable than always landing on your feet.

Love,
Loli

Name: Loli
Age: 10 Years
Re: I'm the only father he's ever known

Name: Blixa, Tiramisu, and Zabaglione
Age: 3 Months
Re: Don't adopt us just because you miss your grandfather

Dear Potential Purchaser of Many Cotton Swabs,

We know it's adoption day, and you're here to take one of us home. That's why you keep staring. It's okay, we know you've never seen anything quite as beautiful as Sphynx kitties. Most people find us so stunning, they can't even believe we're cats. Believe it or not, some humans are jealous, and refuse to admit how cute we are. They call us meowing rats! But don't let the deep wrinkes on our foreheads fool you—we're not worried. We know we're special. And once people have us around their house for a while, they'll see that we're nothing to sneeze at. Mostly because we're hypoallergenic.

Love,
Blixa, Tiramisu, and Zabaglione

Dear My Beloved Crazy Cat Lady,

Normally, a kitty would never share his human. But I'm a little worried about you ever since you tried to take me as your plus one to your cousin's wedding. I think you might need some companionship that doesn't use a cat box. As you can see, I am a great kisser and a master seducer. Once I rub my gums on this cold piece of iron, I will have ruined it for all other cats. And lucky for you, I can also seduce humans. Let me give you some tips.

    First, walk toward the human you want. Then stop for no reason. If you are in heat, howl. But don't howl like you do in the shower, or he'll think you're injured and want you to hide under the couch until you die. Next, keep walking toward him, until you're about a foot away. When he reaches for you, just flop down on your back. Let him scratch your belly for a second—just a taste!—then suddenly bite him. Finally, get up, and weave your way through his legs. Trust me, this drives humans mad. He might even fall head over heels for you right there.

Love,
Bubba

Name: Bubba
Age: 8 Years
Re: Don't be so cold, baby

Name: Muffin
Age: 1 Year
Re: I'd be lion if I said I liked it

Dear Slave to Feline Fashion,

We kitties allow you to share our homes, occasionally open our hearts to you, and thoughtfully try to bury any food we don't like by scraping in vain at the wooden kitchen floor. And what's our thanks? Being humiliatingly shaved to resemble a lion! You wonder why kitties occasionally take up with zoo gorillas. That's because they respect fur. And no zoo gorilla ever thought we'd look cuter pretending to be one of our cat cousins. How would you like it if I asked you to wear your hair like your hotter younger sister? Sure, I'd tell you that I want you to cut your hair so you'll stay cooler in the summer, or keep your hair from matting. But you'd know the truth: I am just entertaining myself by shaving your butt.

Conditional love,
Muffin

Dear Door Opener,

Hey, I didn't expect to see you. Where's Boots? He usually comes to this window so we can hiss at each other. Can you ask him if he can come out and play—or at the very least look at me and arch his back? Pleeeease . . . I have no one to play with today. I promise we won't fight. You won't have to separate us. And after a while of howling, we'll even sit awkwardly near each other on your front steps. The arrogant birdies won't play with me. I think the jingle of my collar adds a nice backbeat to the sound of frantically screeching blackbirds. But they leave before I can even extend my paw in eating—er, I mean, greeting. And the other neighbor's dog is in the house, so I can't walk along the back fence to antagonize him.

Well, at least tell Boots I stopped by—or I can leave him my number in your garden.

Love,
Mia

Name: Mia
Age: 6 Years
Re: Can your cat come out and hiss?

Name: Charlie
Age: 16 Months
Re: I know you said "in the door," but where?

Dear Soon-to-Be Floor Mopper,

I know you said it's "in the door, under tinfoil." But where? There are, like, three things covered in foil, and there are two shelves in the door. Care to be more specific? Just because my eyes glow at night doesn't mean I have X-ray vision. I know you think kitties are lower maintenance than doggies, but that doesn't mean you can be vague about where my can of food is. How would you like it if I were vague about where my litter box was? And speaking of litter boxes, maybe I'd be able to smell which one's the cat food if my box weren't a foot away from the fridge. All I can smell is that you seem to have lost your clump scooper. How can you put my potty in the kitchen, and then get angry when I drink from the toilet? I mean, it's not like you care about hygiene—you've got a cat in your refrigerator.

Love,
Charlie

Dear Distracted Human Male,

You know, most kitties only stand on two feet to watch a bird through a window, or sniff a treat. But I'm doing it because I have to compete with Little Miss Biped behind me. You may think I seem needy or attention starved for standing on two feet for a few seconds, but she is always standing on two feet. Do you really want someone who is too insecure to get down on all fours for you? Sure, I might follow you into the bathroom and try to sit on your lap while you poop. But that's just so you know I care. Do you think she'd do that? Do you think she'd sleep on your face the way I would? A woman like that won't be happy eating from a can every night. But I'll come running the minute you crack the seal. Plus, she has no whiskers. She'll bang into stuff at night and wake you up.

   I think it's obvious who can make you happier. Please don't make me beg.

Love,
Jillian

Name: Jillian
Age: 3 Months
Re: How much do you think I can stand?

Name: Isaac

Age: 7 Years

Re: Sorry I barfed on your bed (the bathroom rug is my
preferred location)

Dear Stain Pretreater,

Thank you for running in here after hearing my prebarf howl, but I'm afraid you're too late. There will be no, "Quick, grab the kitty and put him in the yard!" this time. And although it is most unkitty-like to apologize for anything, I am sorry I barfed on your bed. I was sleeping on it, and now I have to get up. For that, I am truly sorry.

In the future, I will make more of an effort to barf in the appropriate place, such as on the bathroom rug. That way you'll have a nice present to step into barefoot in the middle of the night. I don't know why this barf snuck up on me so quickly. Maybe I caught a bug?

Love,
Isaac

Dear Client,

Let's see, how many pieces do you have? Three shirts, a pair of sweats . . . good, and wow, a ton of socks! I can definitely shed on all of this. Come back after you've sat on the couch for an hour and warmed it up. I will take your place on the warm spot and your clothes in this basket will be ready for pickup. If you need anything starched, please let me know now so I can cough up a wet hairball. Whatever piece of clothes it dries on will be nice and stiff. Also, if you still feel there is not enough of my fur on the clothes once they've been folded, just leave them on the bed, and I will sleep on them again. I promise not to get off until they're so furry they look like a human cat costume, even if that means repeatedly jumping back onto your clean clothes every time you throw me off.

Love and that will be $3.95,
Maggie

Name: Maggie
Age: 2 Years
Re: The laundrocat: Where every coat is a fur coat

Name: Daisy

Age: 5 Years

Re: How do you expect me to get through the day on only twelve hours of sleep?

Dear Provider of Turn-down Service,

No, I'm not getting out of bed. I have accommodated your weird habit of sleeping only at night for far too long. Every kitty knows you should sleep during the day, so at night you can scare children by pawing open cabinets and making them think the house is haunted. Nighttime is for spazzing out and knocking vases off of tables. The only time I hear you spaz out at night is when you have another human sleep over.

And what's with only getting eight hours of sleep? Don't you know the daily minimum is sixteen? No wonder your legs and armpits keep losing all their fur. Every time you start to grow a nice coat, the phone rings, and you say, "Yes, I'd love to go out." Then I follow you into the bathroom to watch you shower, and suddenly all your fur is gone! You should be in bed sleeping two-thirds of your life away like me. And who is rude enough to call at four o'clock in the afternoon—don't they know it's nap time?

Love,
Daisy

Dear Clump Scooper,

At first I was excited. You picked me up, and scratched me on my head, and I was a happy Cherry kitty. Then you brought me into the kitchen, and I thought, "I must be getting a treat for being so adorable." And then the water started running. "I'm not thirsty," I meowed. But I guess you don't speak cat. So, I tried sign language, and flailed my paws in the kitty sign for, "Stop. That is a lot of water, and I am a little kitten." But you didn't get the message. I tried biting your hand and scratching, but it was too late. Not too late for me, that is . . . too late for you.

Sleep with your eyes open,
Cherry

Name: Cherry
Age: 5 Weeks
Re: Worst spa treatment ever

Name: Macho
Age: 15 Years
Re: Dude, it's medicinal

You wanna know why I eat grass? Because sometimes I just can't deal with life, okay! Some days my hairballs are just bringing me down, and all I want to do is cough them up. So, yeah, I have a little grass. It helps with the nausea—by which, I mean it makes me nauseous enough to finally throw up the blockage. You say the grass makes me antisocial, but hey, do you really want me sitting on your lap when I'm about to puke a spring roll? You should lighten up, dude. I know I feel much lighter after a good, grass-fed barf. Maybe you should try it sometime.

Look, I know you love me. You're just worried that grass is a gateway plant, and before I know it I'll be hanging out with strays and eating poinsettias. But if you tried grass, you'd see that it also helps with constipation and provides essential nutrients. Poinsettias are toxic to kitties; I'd never touch that stuff. But grass is medicinal, man. They should legalize it.

Love,
Macho

Dear Butt Scratcher,

Thousands of years ago, when kitties first domesticated humans, we did it so that someone would scratch our butts. We also trained you to scoop our clumps and hunt cans of tuna. But scratching our furry fannies is really why we allow you to share our homes. Before you start getting all full of yourself, you should know that my raised tail is not the offer it appears to be. "Elevator Butt" is actually a leftover response from when I was a kitty and my mommy would help me go potty. That's right, Butt Scratcher, you are my very own personal laxative! Though, now it just feels good, and it really doesn't help me go potty. But don't feel bad, Butt Scratcher. When I go potty, I do think of you—especially when it's in the living room while you're away on a business trip.

Love,
Didjeradoo

Name: Didjeradoo
Age: 16 Years
Re: Don't flatter yourself; it's involuntary

Name: Fuzzy Wuzzy
Age: 2 Years
Re: Welcome to the kitty ornithological society

Dear Fellow Bird-Watcher,

I'm so happy you've decided to join me for some bird hunt—er, um, watching. I have a great ~~appetite~~ appreciation for birds. Do you see that beautiful red-headed thing? Well, according to the copy of *Bird Watcher's Digest* (the leading authority on which birdies you should digest), that is called a house finch! You might not recognize it with its head still attached. But that's what they look like before they've been decapitated, gift wrapped, and left on your doorstep. And that over there is a sparrow. You might know it from its common name, "mysterious pile of feathers on the back porch."

Hey, why do you have a jingly collar in your hand? Can't you see I'm trying to get close to nature?

Love but with annoyed tail flickers,
Fuzzy Wuzzy

Dear Bewitched Bed Warmer,

Why is it that every time your mom visits, you vacuum up my shed fur and then lock me in the bathroom? Are you embarrassed to be with me? You know, one day she's just going to have to accept that you're with a black cat. It's the twenty-first century, and she still thinks I'm a witch. If I'm a witch, then why do I run from the broom? Whenever I cross her path, she runs in the opposite direction. All I want to do is rub myself against her legs. Every time I try to show that woman affection, she just sneezes and acts like she'll die if we're in the same room.

I don't completely blame your mom. You never see positive portrayals of black cats on TV. Orange cats are used to sell cat food. And when an orange cat steals lasagna, it's sweet and funny. Orange cats are cute little guys who wear boots. But black cats? We're always demons and witches! That's some racist BS.

Love,
Coco

Name: Coco
Age: 14 Years
Re: It's a black cat thing; you wouldn't understand

Name: Moka
Age: 11 Years
Re: Claw-strophobia

Dear Real Estate Agent,

My previous residence was a laundry basket. But it was lost in Hurricane Cleaning Lady. This box is cozy, though. Is this front window custom? I always wanted a nice view of people I could scratch if they got too close. And you say the previous owner was a microwave oven? I hope it didn't have any pets.

My housing needs are very particular. You see, I have a condition in which I'm deathly afraid of not being in small, confined places. I just can't handle the fear that when I'm not tucked into a tight space, the rocking chair might bite my tail again, or the little human who wears a litter box around his butt will chase me.

This place is perfect. I'll take it! Just tell me where to put my John Hancat. You can even close the lid right now if you want—I don't mind being a shut-in.

Love,
Moka

Dear Baby-Honey-Sweetheart,

Look, love of my nine lives. Hold on. It's not what it seems. I was just gonna pet it. That's why my paw is out. Don't look shocked. I'm not some violent predatory animal. My instinctual desire to smash this bug into goop was the old me. It was the kitten I was before I met you. You changed me. I'm still the same lovable guy you squeeze too tightly when you read romance novels. Do you remember our first date? You held me and I purred, and I licked your toes after you "accidentally" stepped in marinara sauce. That's who I am, babe. Kill this bug? No way. If you really want to know, he was a present for you. I was going to bring him to your front door and ask if we could adopt what was left of him.

You know I love you, baby,
Kitten

Name: Kitten
Age: 10 Months
Re: I never wanted you to see me like this

Name: Snow
Age: 5 Weeks
Re: Chat room? I think you meant "cat room"

Dear Attention Giver,

I'm a very concerned little kitty. I've jumped onto your computer five times in the past twenty minutes, graciously offering to let you scratch my head. Yet every time, you push me off. What could possibly be more interesting than petting me until I inexplicably tire of you, swat your hand, and then run away? What were you about to do? Go onto a social network, maybe a chat room? Don't you know that people get adorable kitties like me so they don't have to have social lives? How can our relationship blossom if you try to develop normal human relationships?

And who is that whisker-faced trollop on your screen? What does she have that I don't? Why don't you stop fantasizing about some cat who doesn't even know you exist, and give me a head scratch. Pleeeease. You feed me, so I care about you a lot. I know that some cats are aloof. But I'm not one to play hard to pet.

Love,

Snow

Dear Nasal Irritant,

As you know, I'm not just a kitty cat. I am an alien from a distant planet sent to Earth to study the effects of sleeping on heating vents. But my work has been disrupted by a series of uncontrollable cat sneezes. And you know what, human? Laughing at me is not helping. You probably think that with all the hair kitties shed, and all the allergy attacks we cause, it serves us right to occasionally have adorable little sneezing fits. But did you know that cat sneezes can actually be the sign of a bacterial infection? That would make sense, since I live with you, and I have never once seen you lick yourself clean. Or the sneezes might be from accidentally getting litter dust up my nose. But I haven't done that since I was a roadie for Faster Pussycat. Plus, I typically poop in the neighbor's vegetable garden.

    No, the reason I am sneezing is because you're wearing too much of that new Kim Kardashian perfume. If you wanted to smell like a feral cat, you should've just asked. I would've been more than happy to spray you myself.

Love,
Tussi

Name: Tussi
Age: 6 Years
Re: You didn't tell me you have humans . . . I'm allergic to humans

Name: Squishie
Age: 4 Years
Re: Signs that a kitty might have an anger management problem

Dear Enabler,

Maybe I do have anger issues. I admit, I can't stop after shredding one square. I go until the roll's completely ripped. If you tried to separate me from the toilet paper, I'd scratch you. I'm hurting the ones I love.

I've been a shred-head for as long as I can remember—and my mommy was also known to be found on the bathroom floor, covered in two-ply. Do you think I should enter a twelve-step program? I'd probably just sit under the steps and swat at people as they walked up.

But you keep putting out fresh rolls, enabling my problem. Please keep the toilet paper in a drawer and out of my sight. Once I see the white stuff I go crazy.

However, maybe I should hide the toilet paper from you. What I do to it isn't nearly as bad as what you do.

One day at a time,
Squishie

Dear Master,

I should've known this day would come. Last night when you were petting me, you said, "Who's a good kitty?" That's how you talk to a dog! Cats don't care if they're good. You clearly want someone who is in constant need of approval. Why don't you just get a dumb doggie, if you want one so much. I'm sure you can find some idiot pooch who will balance food on his nose, or go crazy when you say the word *jogging*. I'm sorry you can't go jogging with a kitty. But have you ever thought that with me you don't need to jog—I'm happy ignoring you just the way you are.

Love,

Sugar

Name: Sugar
Age: 3 Years
Re: Why can't you love me for who I am?

Name: Biscuit
Age: 1 Year
Re: Bartender, what do you have on tap?

Dear Bartender,

I heard the water running and decided to drop in to the sink for happy hour. Yes, I will have a drink, thank you. Whatever you have on tap is fine. When I was a young kitten and didn't know any better, I would drink from my water bowl. It's all I could get my paws on (which made quite a mess). But it's so stale tasting compared to a sip right from the source. Plus, once in a while when I go to the water dish, there's another cat in the bowl who stares at me. And he's very protective of his water, because the closer I get, the closer he gets. He's fast, too, because when I swat at him he immediately disappears.

But I like what you did with this place. I think this used to be a bathtub, right? That place sucked. I'm glad they pulled the plug on that joint.

Oh what, closing time already? That's fine. I know the bathroom faucet will open for after-dinner drinks.

Love,
Biscuit

Dear Cat Startler,

What is it? Do I have something on my face? Why are you laughing? I was going to do something, but now I can't remember what it was. Don't you hate that? Since I am a cat, and I'm not asleep, I was probably licking myself and forgot to put my tongue back in my face. Is that why you're laughing at me? You know, if you spent a third of your life grooming, you, too, would occasionally forget to pull your tongue back in. And imagine the look on your face if someone walked in on you licking yourself. Your tongue would be the last thing you'd think about putting away. And you would certainly hope they didn't have a camera.

Now, if you'll excuse me, I still have to wash behind my tail—and I don't think you want a picture of that.

Love,
Tasha

Name: Tasha

Age: 1 Year

Re: I'm glad my short-term memory problems amuse you

Name: Calvin
Age: 2 Years
Re: I am King Calvin, but you may call me Lord John

Dear Subjects to the Throne of Calvin,

It is an honor to be your king. And let me say that I was not born as your furry highness, eye level to the toilet paper roll, surveyor of all sinks that drip. I was once a common box user. I know what it's like to toil and bury, to go to sleep with clay under my claws. But no more am I banished to a stinky corner of the garage! I have risen up, and in so doing released my subjects from the feudal tyranny of scooping clumps. To celebrate, we will have games. Subjects, fetch me your finest string!

Love,
King Calvin the 1st
and 2nd

Dear Bringer of Pests,

You see this dead mousy? This is what happens when you cross Marko's floor without saying, "Hi, Marko kitty," and scratching my head. I know you might be tempted to remove the body, but don't! Another mousy looking and smelling exactly like him will just show up tomorrow, and I'll have to kill him all over again. I don't know how the exact same mousy keeps reappearing, but I'm a busy kitty, and I have socks to chew through and tinfoil balls to knock under the couch. I can't spend every day killing a mousy I could swear I already killed. So please, leave it out to remind the mouse that he is actually dead, and I'm bored with him.

Love,
Marko the Magnificent

Name: Marko
Age: 2 Months
Re: Let this be a warning to your toes

HUGE THANKS

to the extremely talented photographers who blessed this book with their work:

DOGS

Valerie Abbott, Marley, page 18; Amy Burgess, Dodger, page 49; Alana Carlin, Jasper, page 29; Ruth Cassidy, Doesn't Like Dress-up, page 41; Robert Counselman, Max, page 54; Michael Culver, T-Bone, page 42; Elaine Dudzinski, Ozzy, page 33; Cindy Fike, Kellan, page 17; Peta Flemming, Samson, page 9; Jennifer Heffner, Samuel, page 45; Carolyn Abell Hodges, Macy, page 26; Davee Hughes, Frogdog, page 25; Peggy Hughes, Mario, page 34; Lin Jia, Gandalf, page 10; Erin Leonard, Raisin, page 62; Caroline Li, Mousse, page 50; Matt Mallett, Bernie, page 37; Sarah Novak, Jane, page 30; Jodi Payne, Sammy, page 38; Ellen Pierce, Doll, page 58; Rebecca Pizzo Photography, Mr. P Nut, page 14; Paula Rivas, Biting the Colors, page 21; Kathleen Slovachek, Dante, page 61; Marshall Stokes, Stella, page 53; Renee Tellez, Mel, page 22; Reggie Thibodeau, Jewel, page 13; Valerie Trinidad, Babe, page 57; Bernadette Walsh, Spike, page 46; Marit Welker, Sukie, page 6.

CATS

Carter Belleau, Moka, page 102; Elizabeth Blake, Isaac, page 86; Catherine Chanel, Coco, page 101; CitiKitty Pet Products, Calvin, page 118; David Clemmons (spacemouses), Kitten, page 105; Betsy Cole, Muffin, page 78, and Cherry, page 93; Dave DeHetre, Marko, page 121; Joan De Lurio, Didjeradoo, page 97; Sandy Ellis, Bubba, page 77; Fearon-Wood Photography, Fuzzy Wuzzy, page 98; Carolyn Ganus, Biscuit, page 114; Linda M. Goodman, Daisy, page 90; William H. Haas, Jillian, page 85; Staffan Hamnas, Tussi, page 109; Jason Hitchens, Maggie, page 89; Andrey Hristov, Charlie, page 82; Marjorie Lear, Macho, page 94; Loriann Morris, Squishie, page 110; Leta Paine, Tippy, page 66; Jodi Payne, Tasha, page 117; Edward H. Pien, Mia, page 81; Niklas Pivic, Blixa, Tiramisu, and Zabaglione, page 74, and Hendrix, page 65; Paula Rivas, Loli and the Teddy Bears, page 73; Peder Sandholm, Ili, page 70; Jaret Segovia, Dakota, page 69; Jixue Yang, Snow, page 106; Jia Zhang, Sugar, page 113.

ACKNOWLEDGMENTS

First and foremost, allow me give the absolute highest thanks again to this book's brilliant editor, Lane Butler, for believing in my profound mission to make fun of stuff. Also, a world of thanks to my awesome agent, David Fugate, for insisting I pitch this idea. Super huge thanks to Caty Neis for graciously reading gazillions of e-mails and helping me evaluate photos; to Kathy Hilliard for her outstanding promotional work; and to everyone at Andrews McMeel who have again devoted themselves to the creation of another great book!

Very special thanks to everyone at team MSN: to the amazing Gina Cohen and her tireless efforts to build our family of readers; to Nicole Ghazal for getting it all started; and to everyone else at Lifestyle and beyond who have continued to make room for *The Family Room*.

I would further like to thank Amanda Brothers of Sidekick Dog Training, Molly Wyman, my sherpa Chris Federico, Andrew Norelli, Tommy Savitt, and all of my great friends and colleagues!

And, most important, my deepest love and thanks to my beautiful wife, Barbara; our amazing children, Ben and Seth; and my doggie and muse, Dagny.

ABOUT THE AUTHOR

Jeremy Greenberg is an internationally headlining stand-up comedian, author, blogger, and joke writer. He has appeared on numerous national TV and radio shows, and has done six overseas tours to perform for our troops. Jeremy has also been a contributing joke writer for *The Complete Idiot's Guide to Jokes* and *Comics Unleashed with Byron Allen*. And if that weren't enough, he's also the author of *Relative Discomfort: The Family Survival Guide, Sorry I Peed on You (and Other Heartwarming Letters to Mommy)*, and *Manwords: Real Words for Real Men*. Additionally, he is read by millions each day as the blogger for MSN's *The Family Room*, and was part of the team that helped MSN win the 2009 IMA Outstanding Achievement Award for the category of "blogs." When Jeremy is not performing or writing, he is at home in San Diego demonstrating alpha-male behavior to his twin sons—mostly by saying "Whatever" and leaving the room every time his wife says that he's incorrectly loaded the dishwasher. Learn more at www.sorryibarfedonyourbed.com.

Andrews McMeel Publishing, LLC
an Andrews McMeel Universal company
1130 Walnut Street, Kansas City, Missouri 64106

www.andrewsmcmeel.com
www.jeremygreenberg.com

15 16 17 18 19 SDB 10 9 8 7 6 5 4 3 2 1

ISBN: 978-1-4494-7372-3

ATTENTION: SCHOOLS AND BUSINESSES
Andrews McMeel books are available at quantity discounts with bulk purchase for educational, business, or sales promotional use. For information, please e-mail the Andrews McMeel Publishing Special Sales Department: specialsales@amuniversal.com.